A Year in Flowers

COLORING BOOK

JESSICA MAZURKIEWICZ

DOVER PUBLICATIONS, INC.
GARDEN CITY, NEW YORK

D1384508

The beauty of nature comes to life in these 31 illustrations of flowers associated with each birth month. From the carnations and snowdrops of January to the roses of June and the marigolds of October, the delicately drawn blossoms and blooms reflect traditional birthday flowers. Inspiring quotations add to this dazzling collection, along with seasonal sights such as honeybees, pumpkins, and pine cones. Captions identifying the birth-month flowers appear in gray on the back of the illustrations. Experience the glories of nature as you color your special birth flower and those of your loved ones with markers, colored pencils, or any medium of your choice. The pages are perforated for easy removal and display.

Copyright
Copyright © 2021 by Dover Publications, Inc.
All rights reserved.

Bibliographical Note
A Year in Flowers Coloring Book is a new work, first published by
Dover Publications, Inc., in 2021.

International Standard Book Number
ISBN-13: 978-0-486-84719-1
ISBN-10: 0-486-84719-5

Manufactured in the United States by LSC Communications
84719501
www.doverpublications.com

2 4 6 8 10 9 7 5 3 1
2021

WINTER

WINTER IS NOT A SEASON. IT'S A CELEBRATION

—ANAMIKA MISHRA

Flowers

Paperwhites, Poinsettias, Snowdrops, Violets,
Pansies, Irises, Primroses, Snowflakes

Flowers

❧

Carnations, Snowdrops

January
is the
month for
dreaming

—JEAN HERSEY

Flowers

Carnations, Snowdrops

Flowers

Violets, Irises, Primroses

In February there is
everything to hope for
and nothing to regret

—PATIENCE STRONG

Flower

Violets

SPRING

BLOSSOM BY BLOSSOM. THE SPRING BEGINS

—ALGERNON CHARLES SWINBURNE

MARCH

Flower

Daffodils

Oh, the lovely
fickleness of an
April day!

—W. H. GIBSON

Flowers

Daisies and Sweet Peas

MAY

All things seem possible in May

—EDWIN WAY TEALE

Flower

Roses

Flower

Delphinium

Hot July brings cooling showers,
Apricots, and gillyflowers

—SARA COLERIDGE

Flower

Larkspur

Breathe in the
sweetness that hovers
in August

—DENISE LEVERTOV

Flower

Asters

By all these lovely tokens
September days are here
with summer's best of weather
and autumn's best of cheer

—HELEN HUNT JACKSON

Flower

Morning Glories

Flower

Marigolds

I'm so glad I live in a world where there are Octobers

—L.M. MONTGOMERY

Flower

Marigolds

Flower

Chrysanthemums

In November,
the earth
is growing quiet

—CYNTHIA RYLANT

DECEMBER

I heard a bird sing in
the dark of December

A magical thing, and
sweet to remember

—OLIVER HERFORD

Flower

Poinsettias

JANUARY

FEBRUARY

MARCH

APRIL

MAY

JUNE

JULY

AUGUST

SEPTEMBER

OCTOBER

NOVEMBER

DECEMBER

Flowers

Carnations, Violets, Daffodils
Daisies, Lilies of the Valley, Roses
Delphinium, Poppies, Asters
Marigolds, Chrysanthemums, Poinsettias